Daydreams Alongside Surf

Cinquain Magic

by Jim Ross

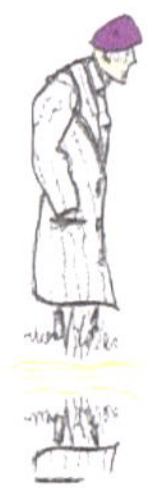

Scriptline Images
Beret Imprint
21740 El Puma Cir
Sonora, CA 95370

Library of Congress Cataloging-in-Publication Data
Ross, Jim (James Lee), 1941—
Daydreams Alongside Surf: poetry

Includes bibliographical references and index.

ISBN: 978-0-9978003-4-0

poetry. 2. cinquain. xxx.x'x—dcxx

BISAC: Poetry / American / General

Dedication

For Jim Newby: they don't make men finer than you

Epigraph

When the sun is right
and the shade protects ones' peace
revelations show
themselves in bits and pieces
gathered by a beating heart

CONTENTS

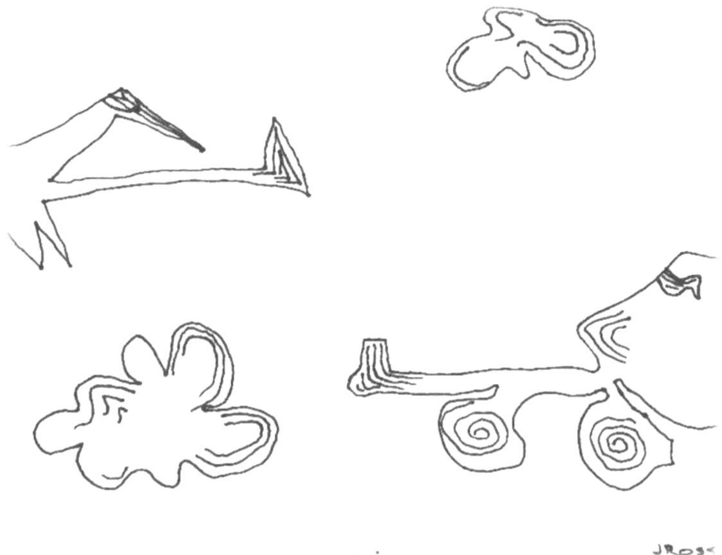

Figure 1--WA-NA-BI

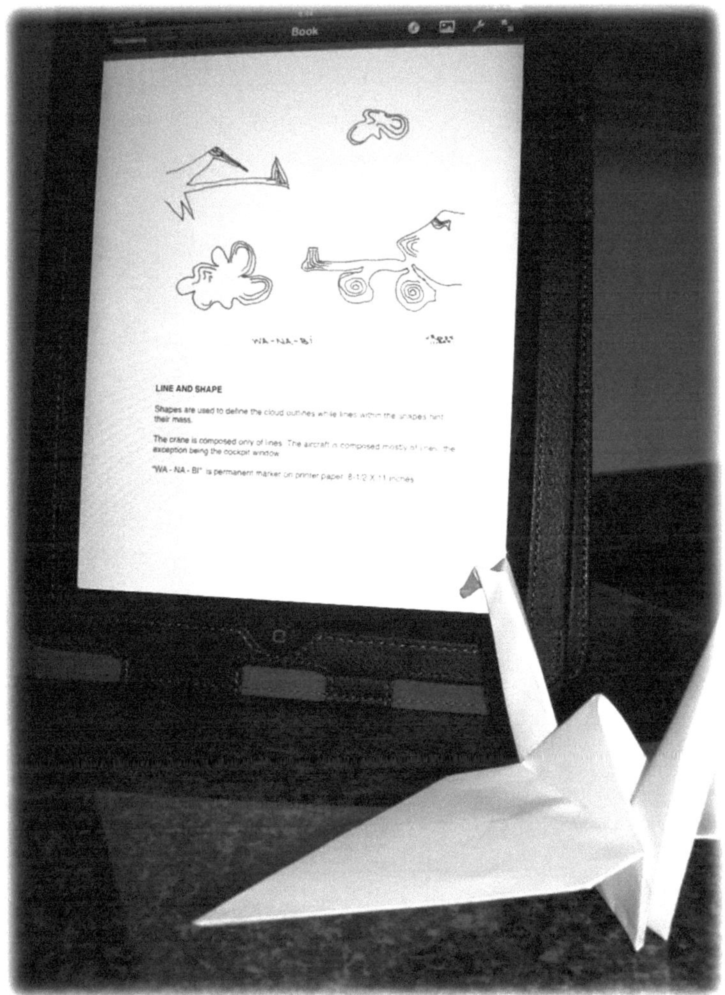

Figure 2--I'M A LEGEND

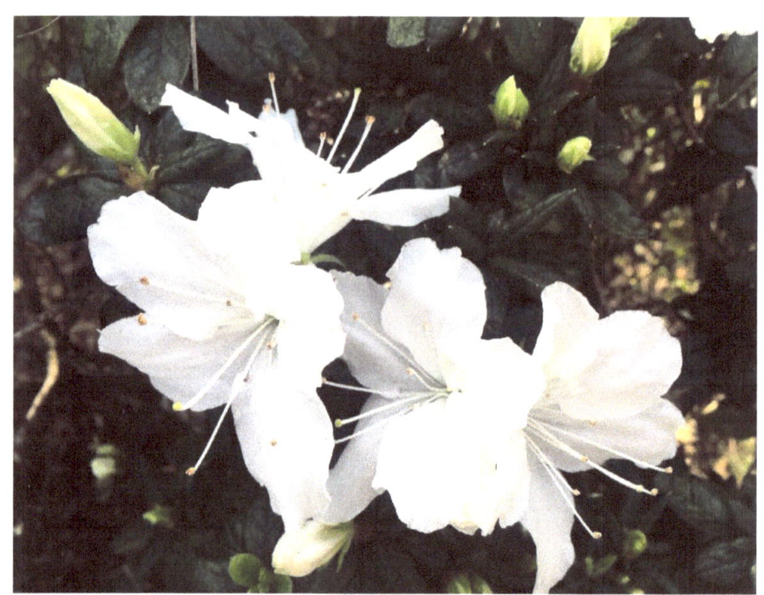

Figure 3--DELICATE

Dance of Spring

Worthy
little flowers
push for places of sun
to unfold their cheerful petals,
flutter
for our delight
across shimmering fields,
into news that translates the word,
"worthy"

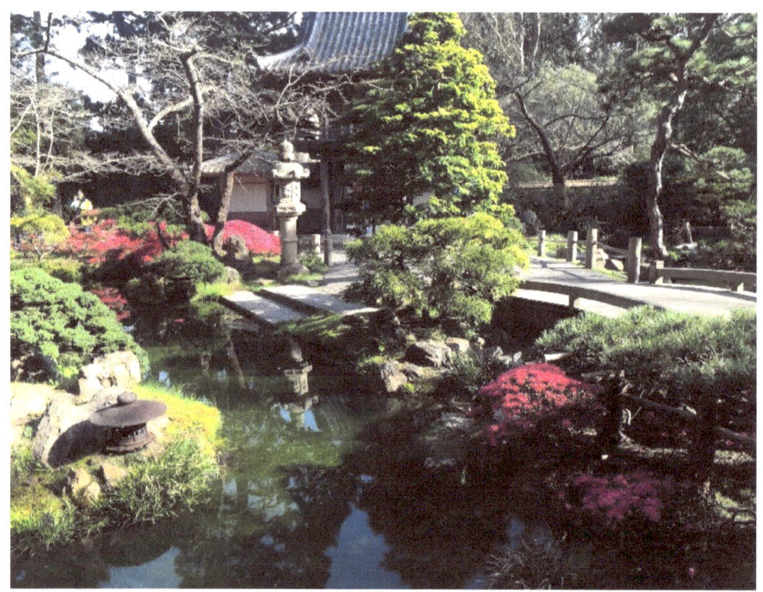

Figure 4--TRANQUILITY

Tickle Time

Sunday
captures my soul
and bathes it in bubbles
that burst and tickle a fancy
day off

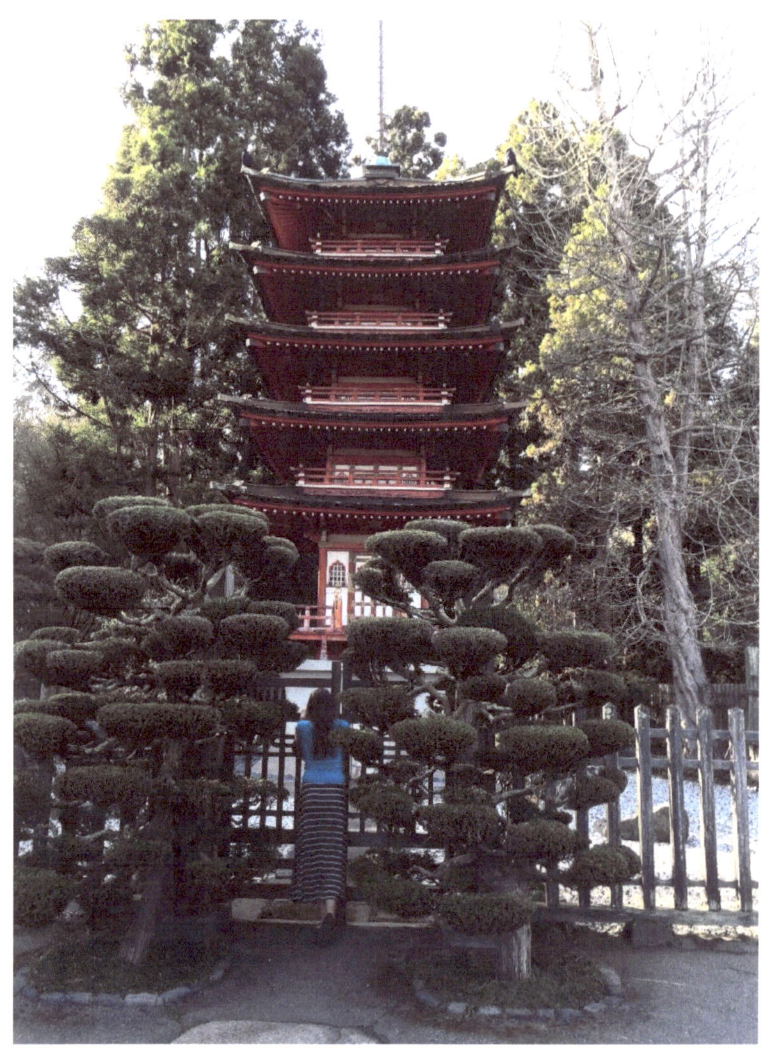

Figure 5--DISCOVERY

Two Times

Two Times
I see you, now
first yearning and growing.
then nourishing the things you
touch
with love

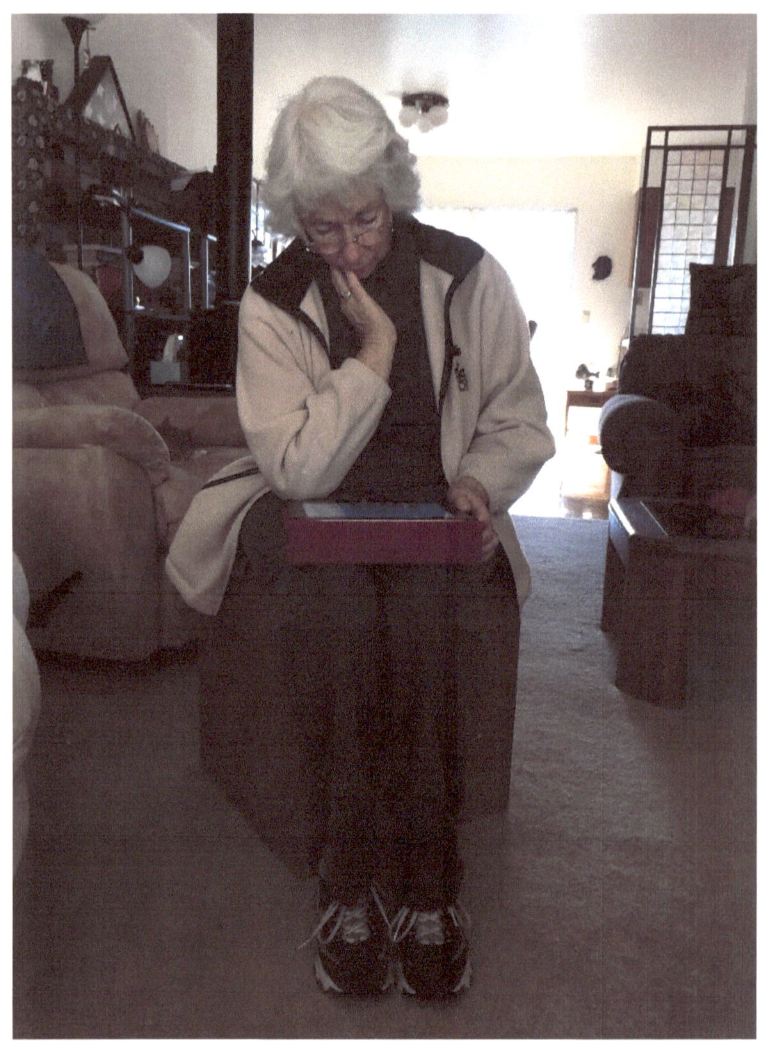

Figure 6--STUDY WHERE YOU CAN

Wisdom

Gracious
is the sovereign
who reflects on her deeds
then passes the adoring throng
with love

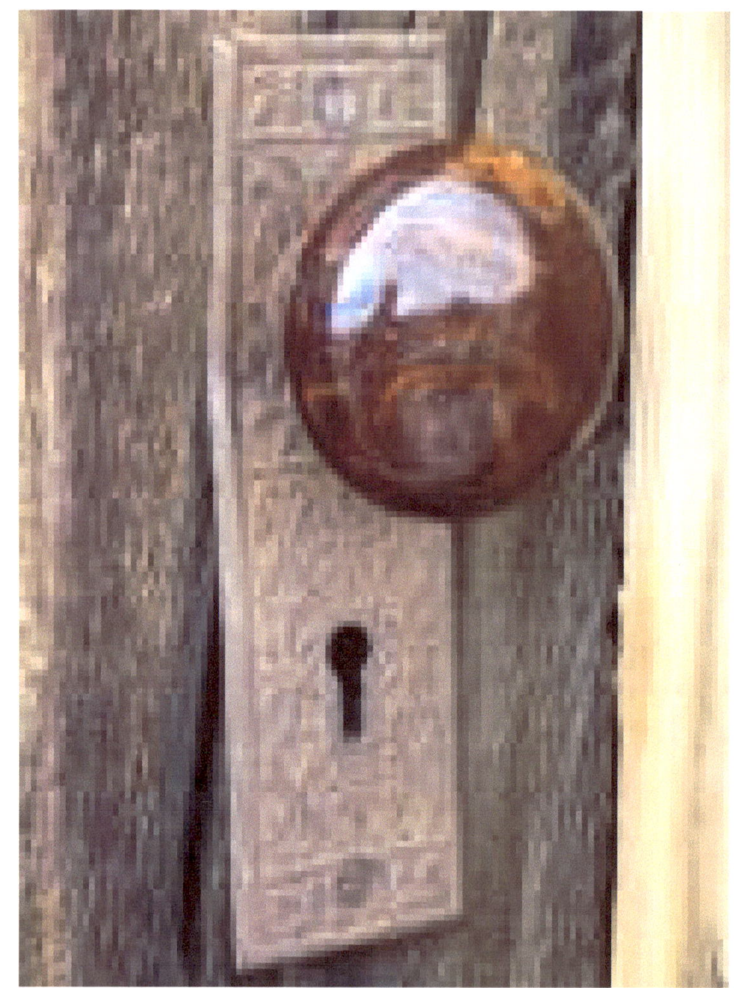

Figure 7--LATCH TO YESTERDAY

Yesterday's Justice

Courtroom
frozen in time
without legal motions
to flutter cobwebs draped on signs,
is "Closed"

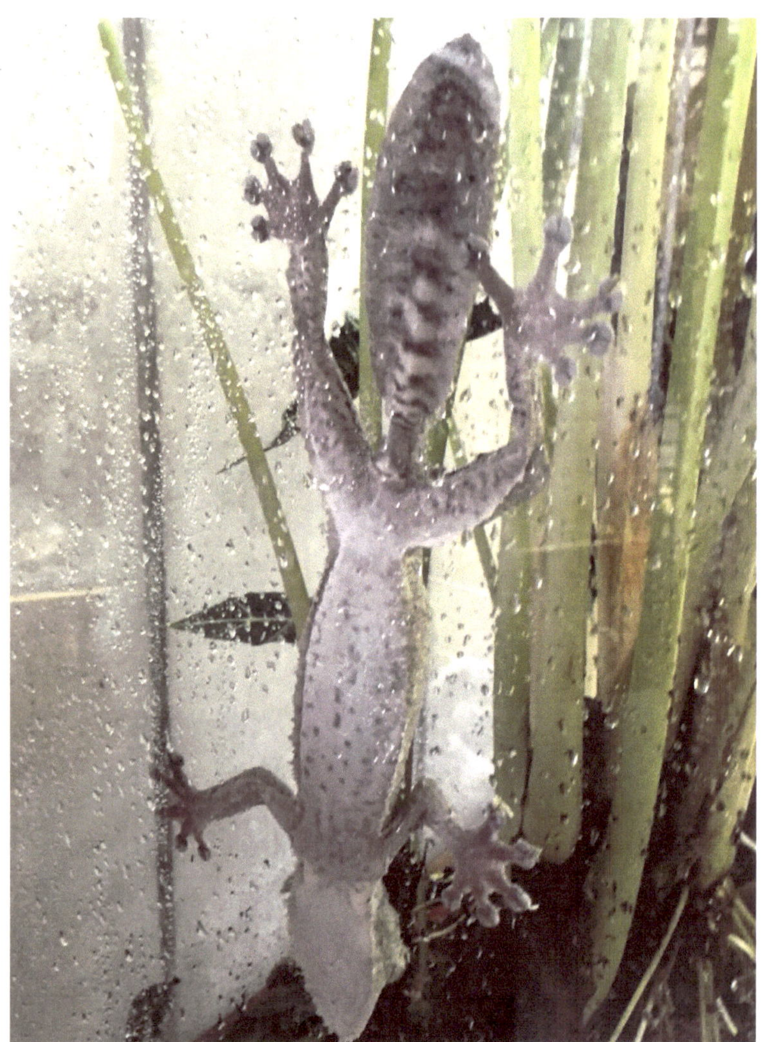

Figure 8--I LIKE THE RAIN

Wild River Veil

Valley
shadows of blue
blacken as the thunder rolls
till river and canyon are one
echo

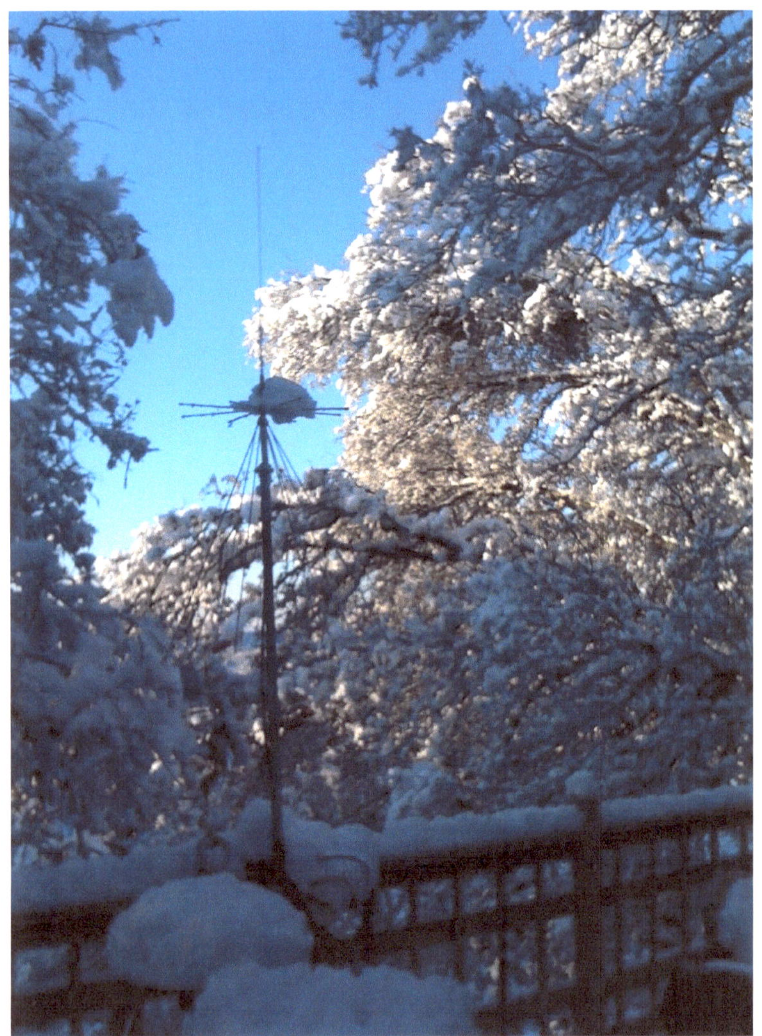

Figure 9-THE WORLD WE SEE . . . AND DON'T

Winter Hunt

Over
the meadow snow
a fox swiftly high-steps,
his bushy tail scraping telltale
paw prints
as he passes,
leaps high over chaos
where the grounded rabbit leaps…
over

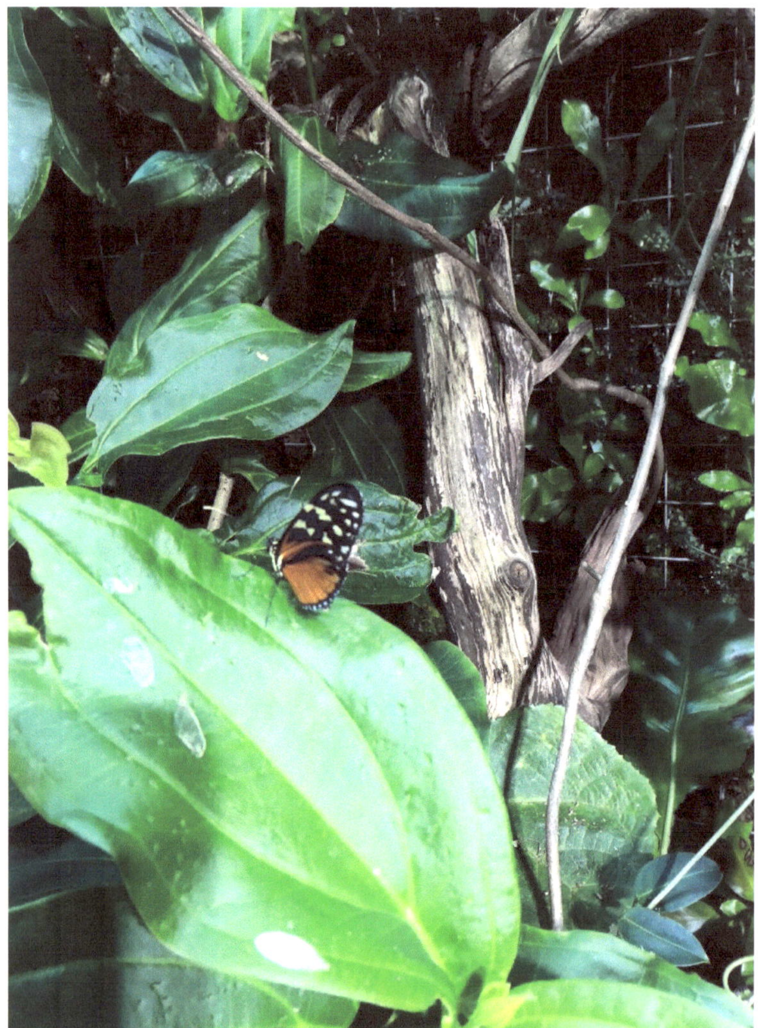

Figure 10--NICE LITTLE BED

More Than A Smile

Paltry
smiles gain nothing
without inspiring words
to silhouette your ample heart
luster

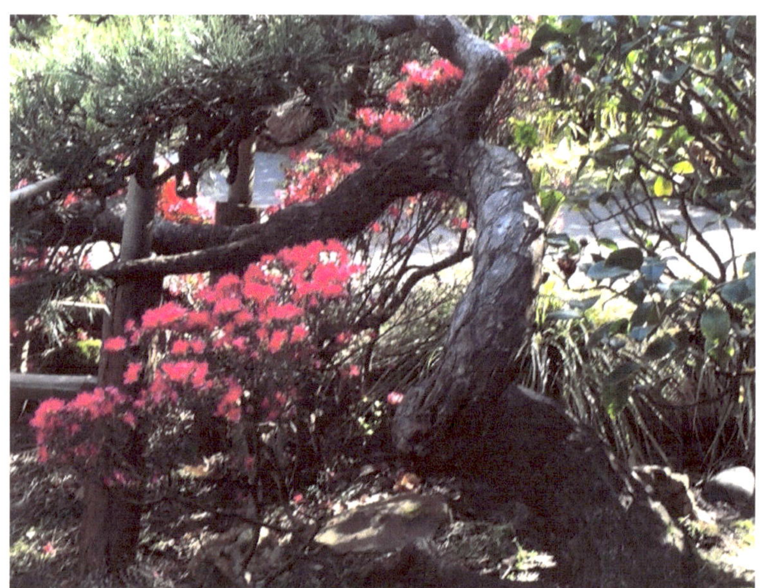

Figure 11—INSPIRATION

Patience

Lovely
buds wait for spring,
gentler climes to unfurl
and swell in new vibrant colors,
to view

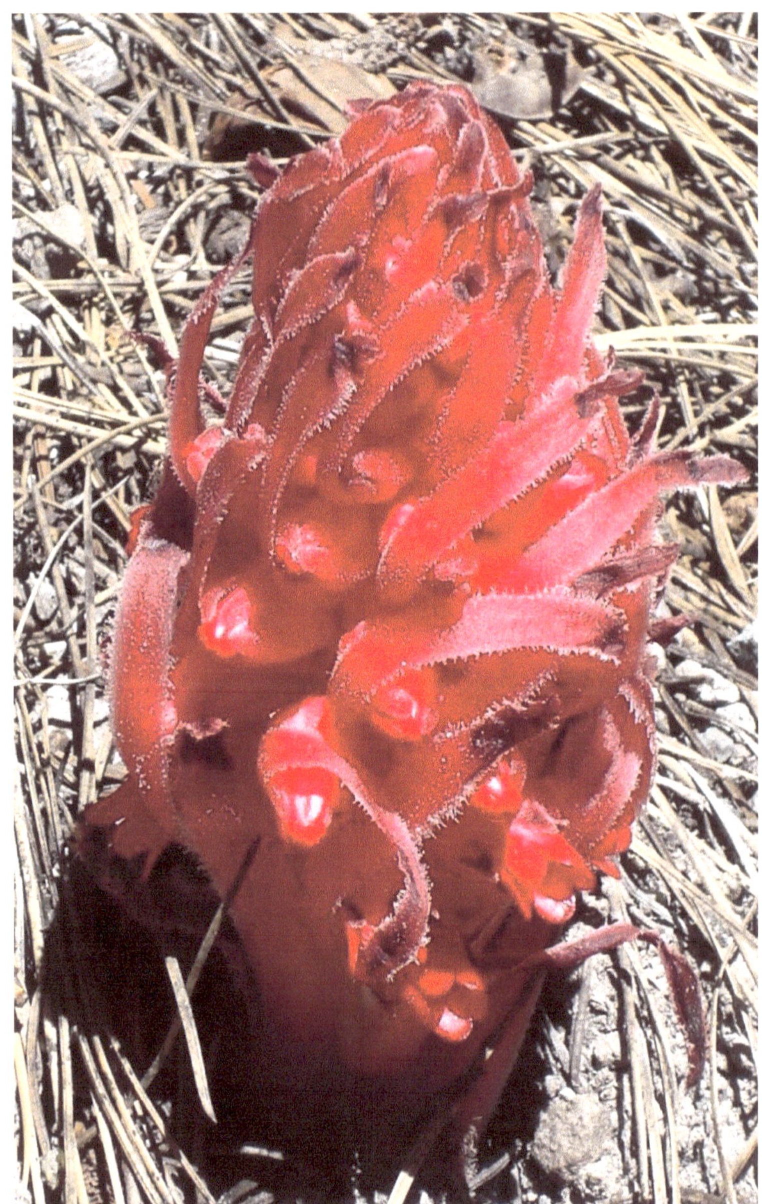

Figure 12--SNOW FLOWER, FLEETING FUNGUS

Bullfight

Crimson
choreographed
cape in cunning pursuit,
reveals its gleaming heart, and
drops,
shivers

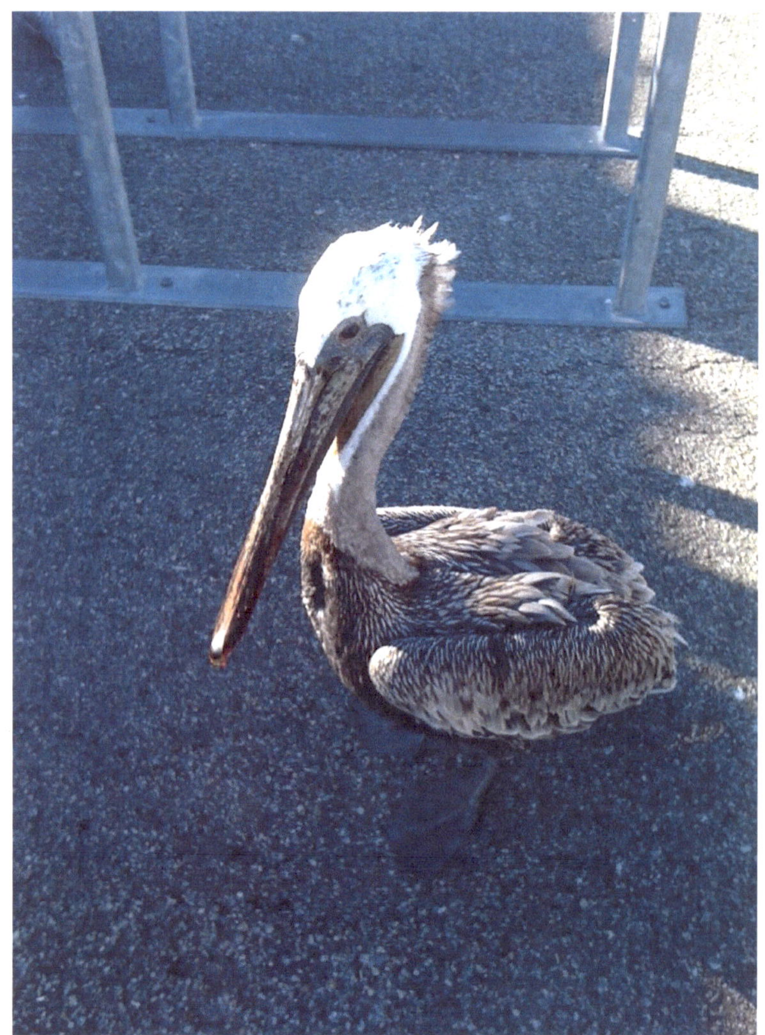

Figure 13--AREN'T I THE HANDSOME STROLLER

Barefoot

Barefoot
fellow follows
trails broadly tamped by carts
in search of a cobbler's comfort—
good shoes

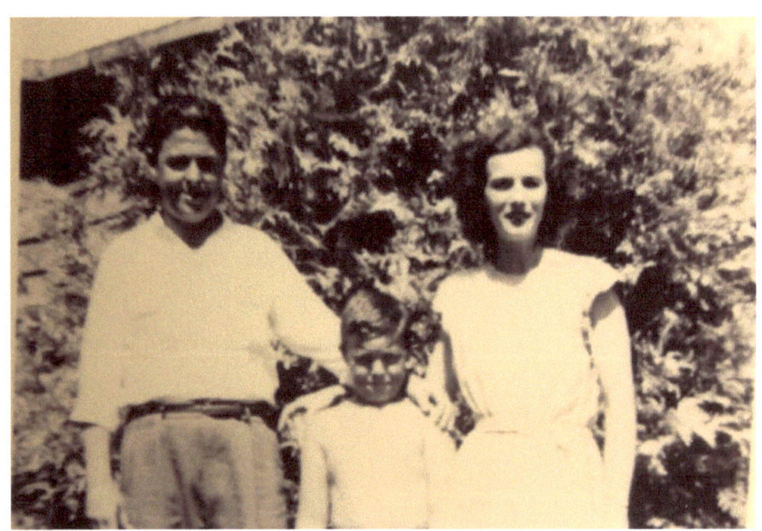

Figure 14--OUT OF THE PAST, NURTURE

Mother and Son: The Truth

"Oh, Mom!"
I see you now
with stern eyes so focused
to watch my every twitching
move—
"I lied."

Father and Son: The Hope

"Hi, Dad—
Mom said tell you
about my breaking faith
and sneaking over to see Barb—
my girl."

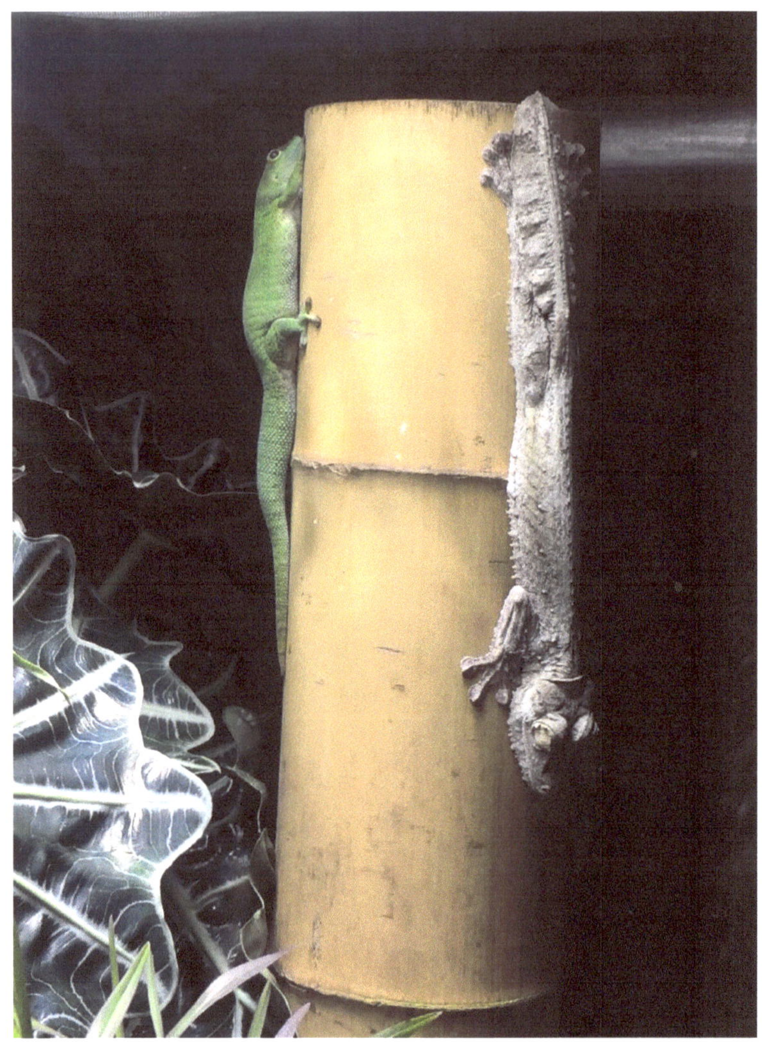

Figure 15--STRANGERS DANCE

Strangers' Dance

A glance,
a modest smile,
a hand to hold and guide
a stranger to the floor of dance
a smile
where music strains
and gently prods your grace
to open to this stranger's soul
and dance

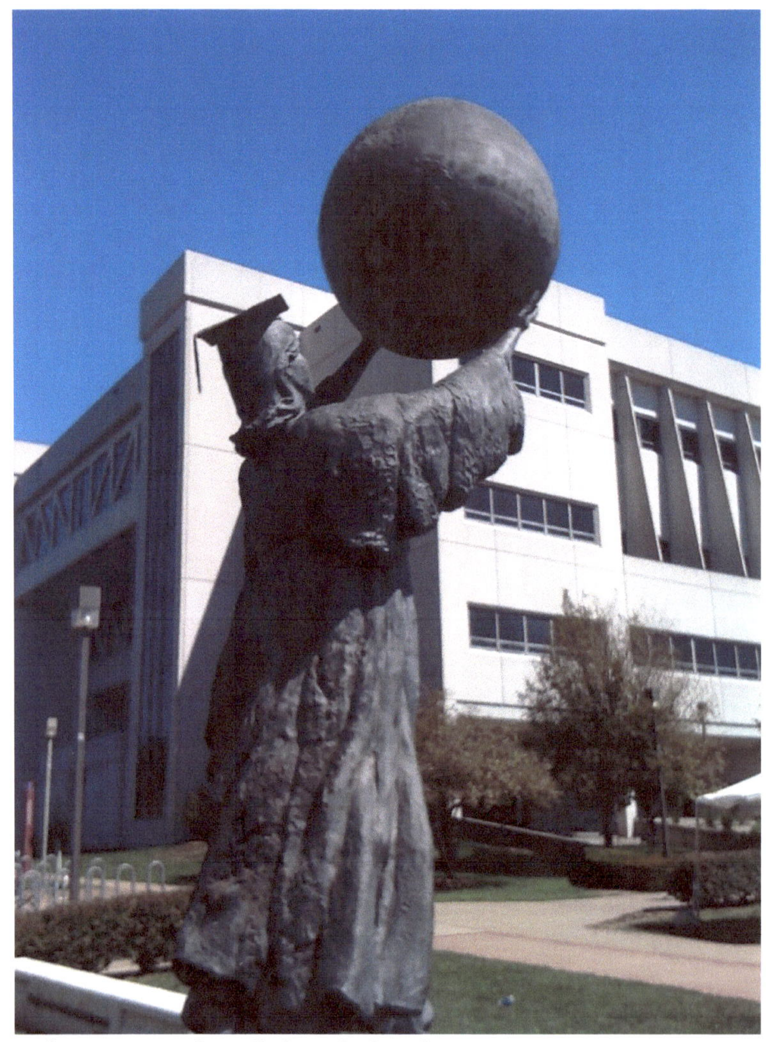

Figure 16--SCHOOLS WERE BUILT AS THE WORLD SPUN

One Small Step…Then Another

Heaven
knows the glory
of spinning, whirling orbs,
while Man unravels grand puzzles
on earth

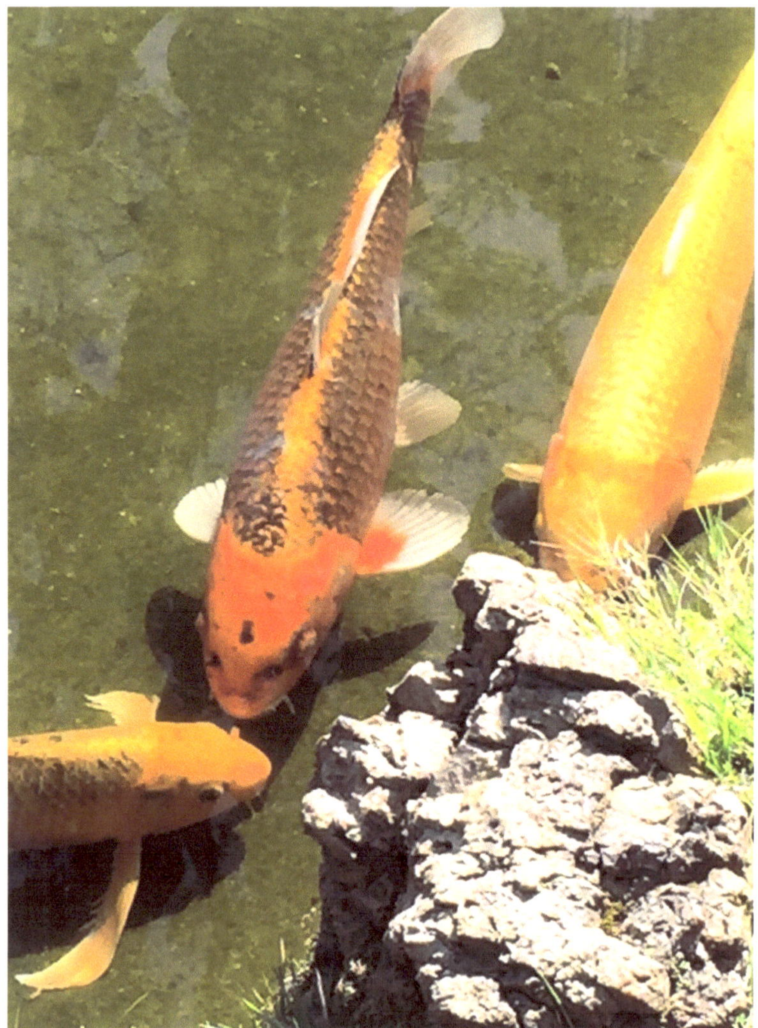

Figure 17--THERE'S MORE CHOW OVER THERE

Sprites and Spring

Sprightly
elusive elves
with grins wide with mischief
dart and share their lively magic in
spring

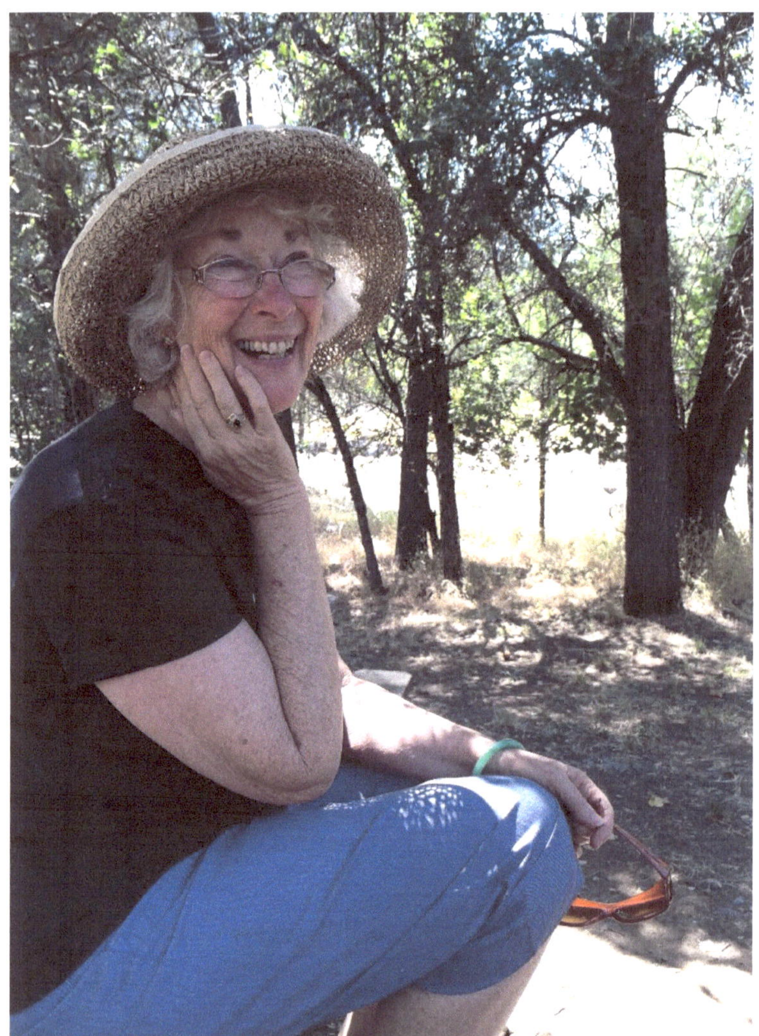

Figure 18--SIMPLY JOY

Moment of Truth

Profile
my heart beating
a tattoo to guide words
that soften your eyes, and win your fondness

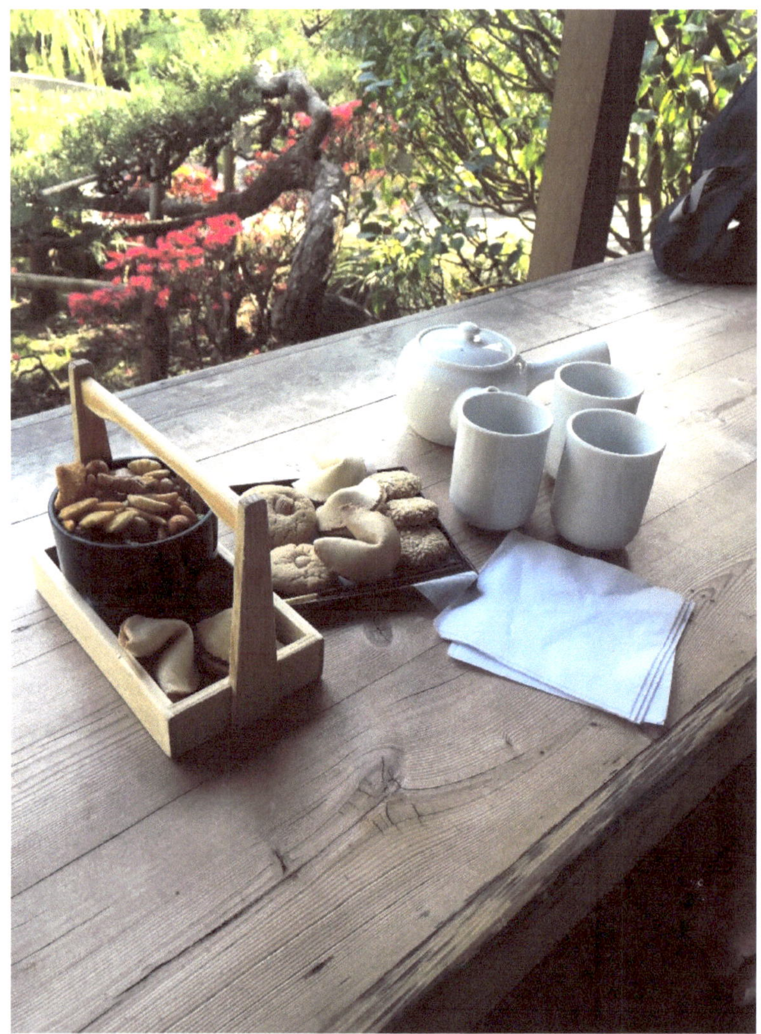

Figure 19--HOT, SWEET, AND REFRESHING

Savory Salsa

A taste
of hot, curried rice,
A glance at your allure
over glasses of vintage wine—
sweat pops

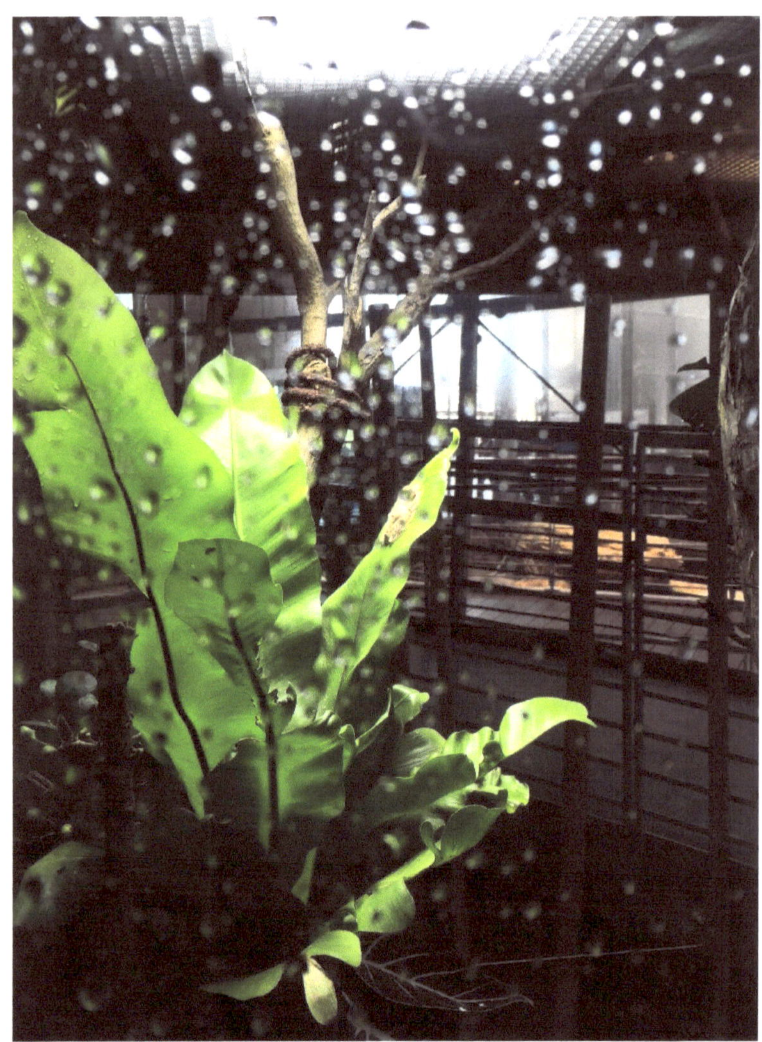

Figure 20--MYSTERIOUS CHEMISTRY

My Place or Yours?

A stroll
down foreign streets
feeling strange ambience
beneath thunderstorms that span
time
and placc

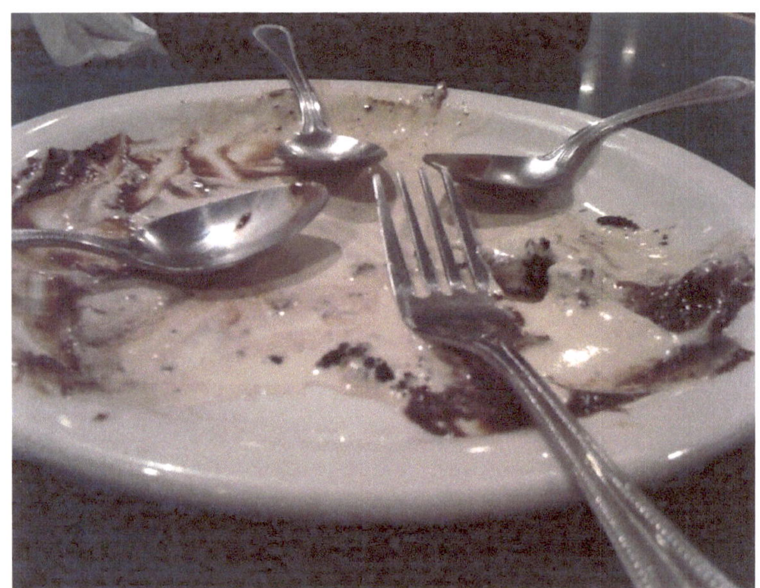

Figure 21--THREE GUESSES: WHO IS ON A DIET?

Mocha

Frothy
milk rims the cup
streams down sides to disclose
hints of delectable chocolate
within

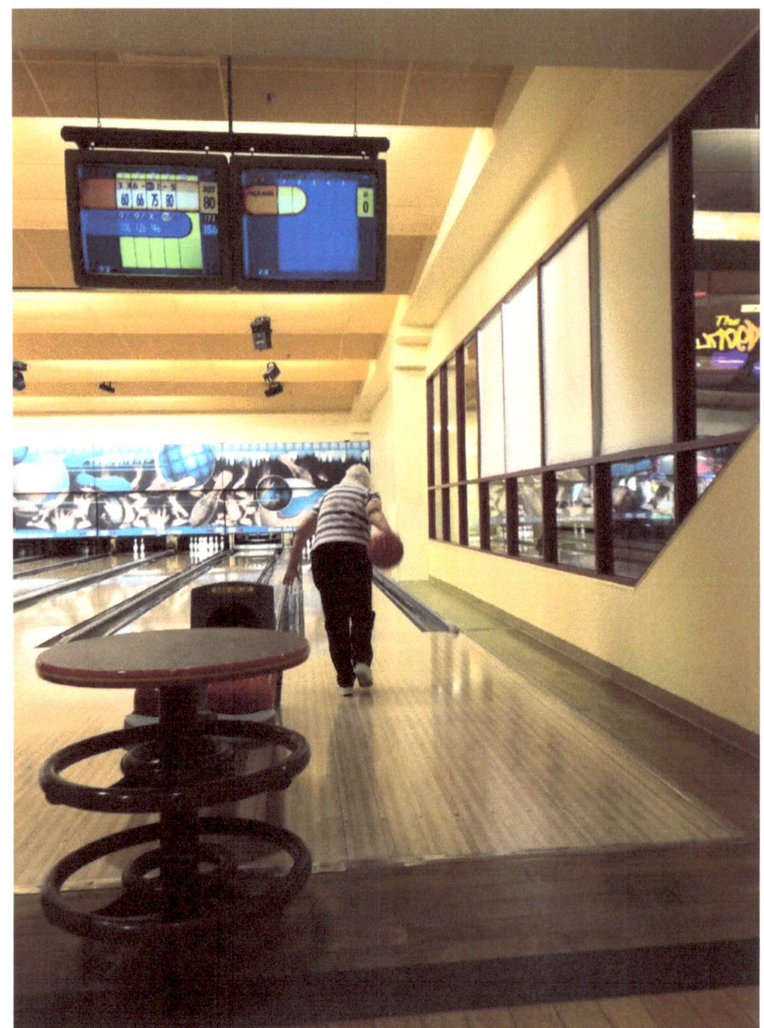

Figure 22--REFRESHING EXERCISE

Exhausted

The bed
with the blanket
stretched loosely across it
beckons my tired eyes to narrow…
come close

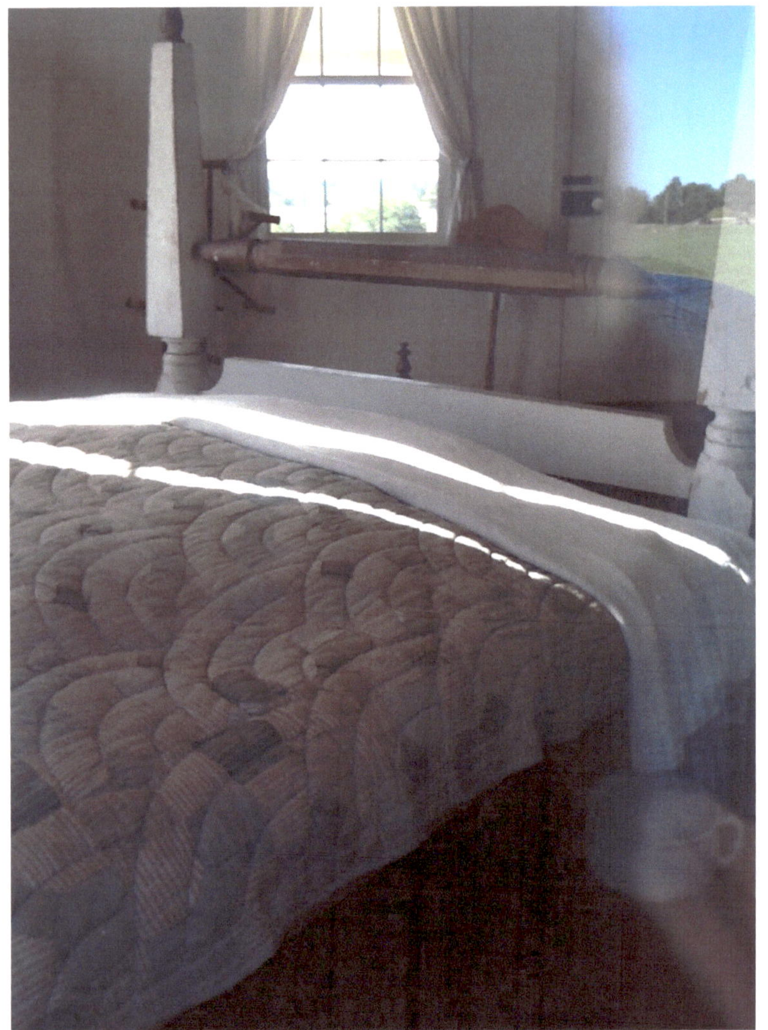

Figure 23--GOOD TO SEE YOU, OLD FRIEND

The Rest

Pillows
serve their purpose
and nest my head resigned
for my hours of solitude
to sleep

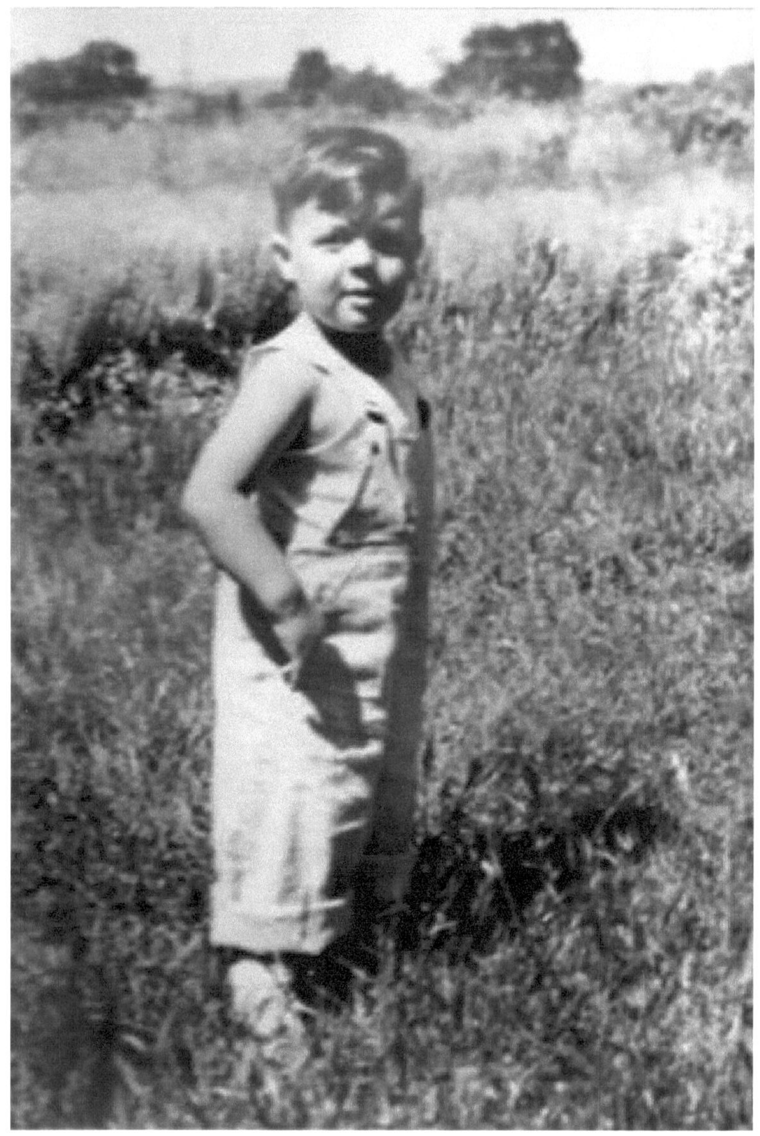

Figure 24--I THINK IT'S THE GRASS

Daily Question

The dawn
with due freshness
awaits my rested eyes
all mystery with no new clues
distinct

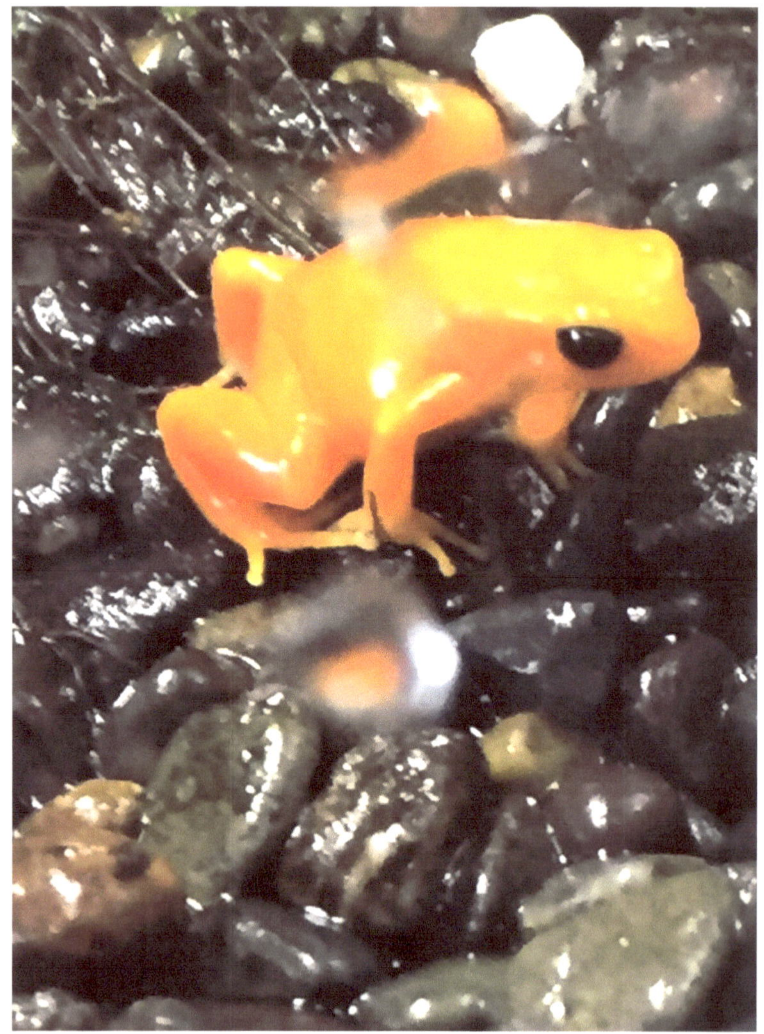

Figure 25--ANYONE TOXIC AROUND HERE?

Dizzy

My heart
spoke to my head
too fast to understand
everything I needed to hear
about you

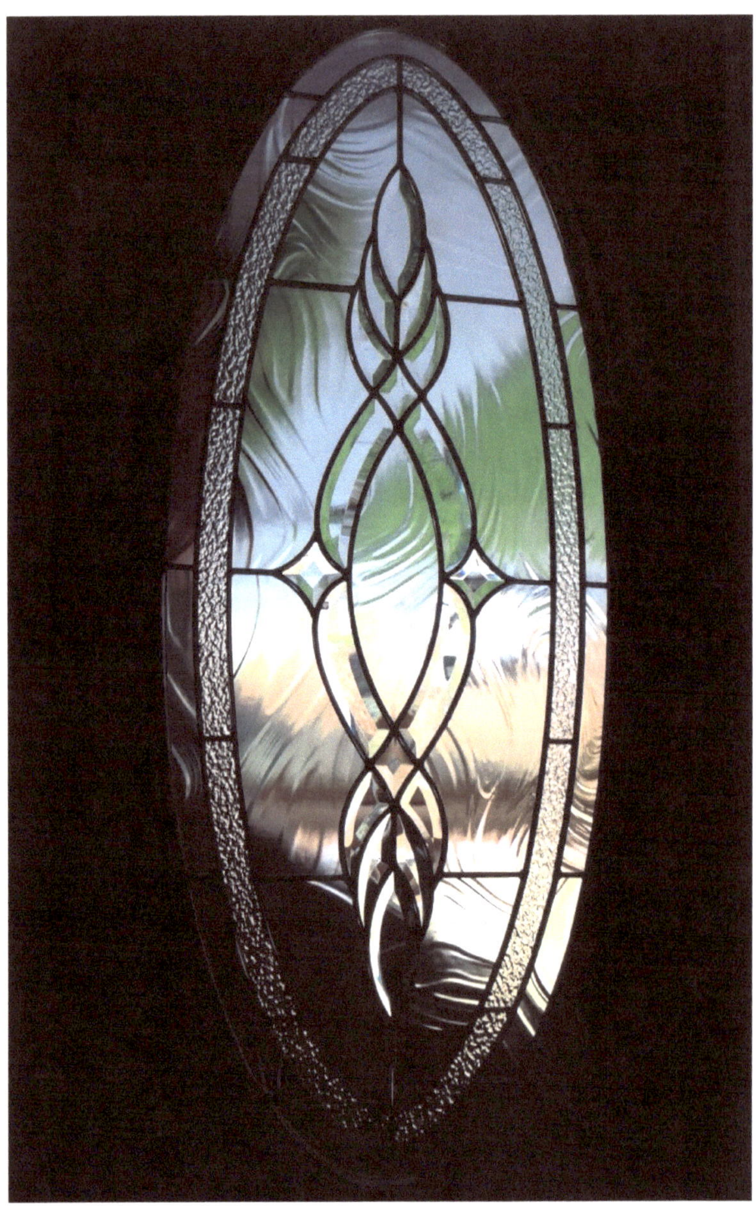

Figure 26—TANTALIZING

Breathless

Breathless
I hear your steps
behind the closed door
and my mind wings through images
replete
with elegance
charming at blazing speed
till the sound of the latch stops
time
Breathless

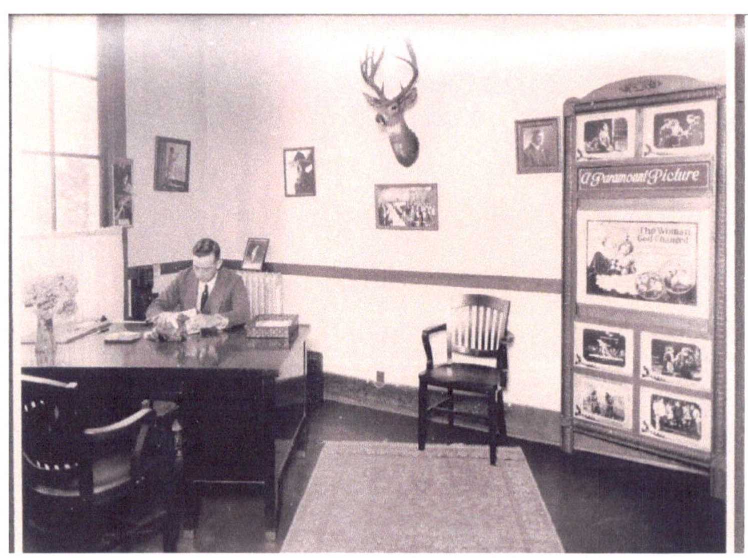

Figure 27--SO, I LOVE THE PICTURE BUSINESS!

I Understand

Chiseled
truth, kindly told,
evokes soft, knowing smiles—
harbingers of common boundary
candor

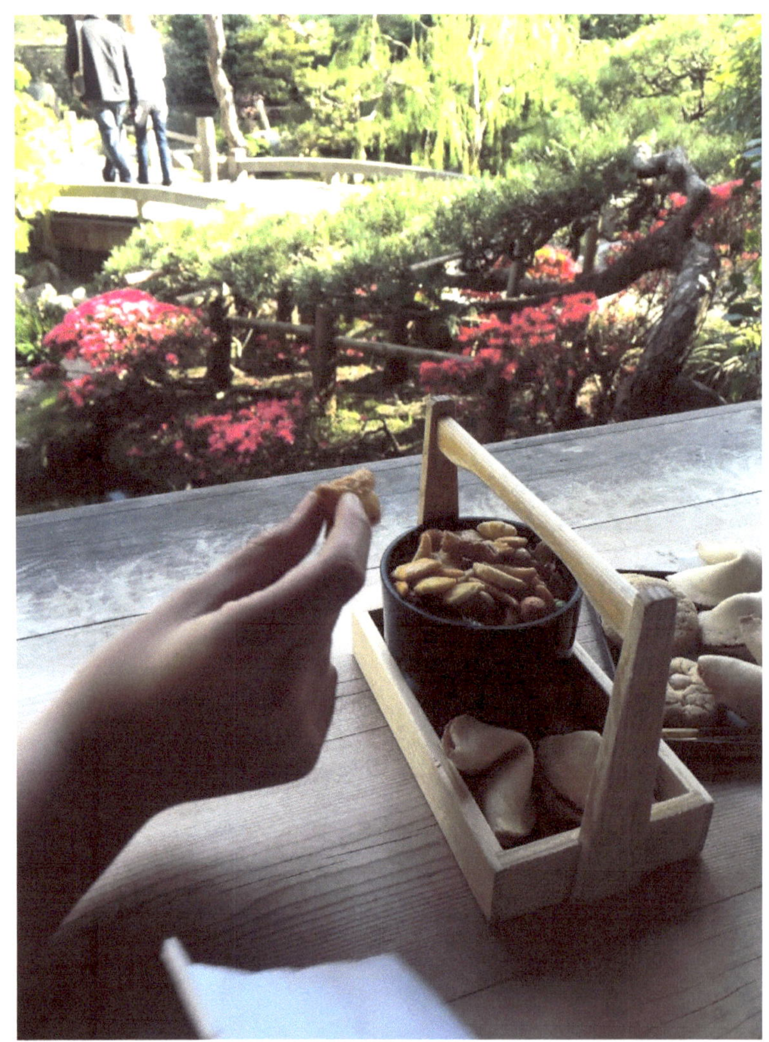

Figure 28--I'M NOT LEAVING HERE, EVER!

Ambience

Garnish
enlivens food
beneath our soft love-talk,
indispensible flavor
for mood

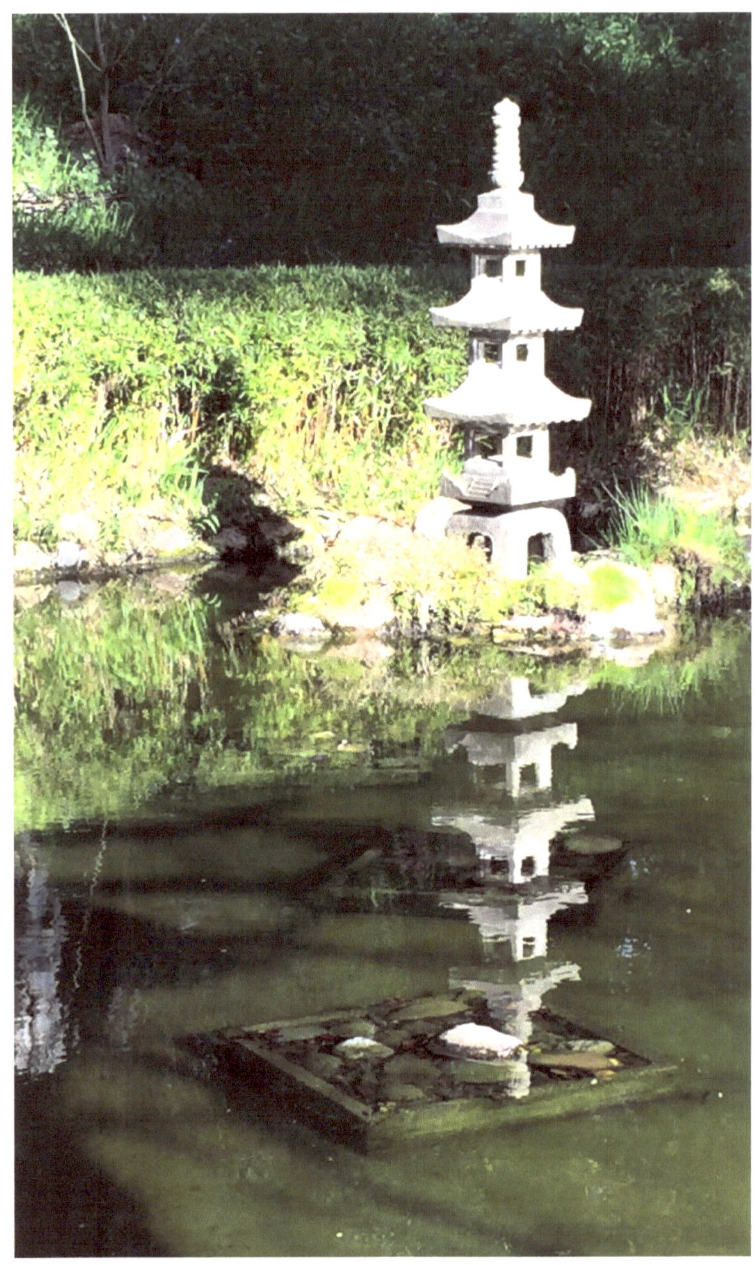

Figure 29--I'LL FIND YOU

Dream Come True

A kiss,
enamored one
of my enchanted dream,
whose eyes meet mine with peace
and joy,
is mine

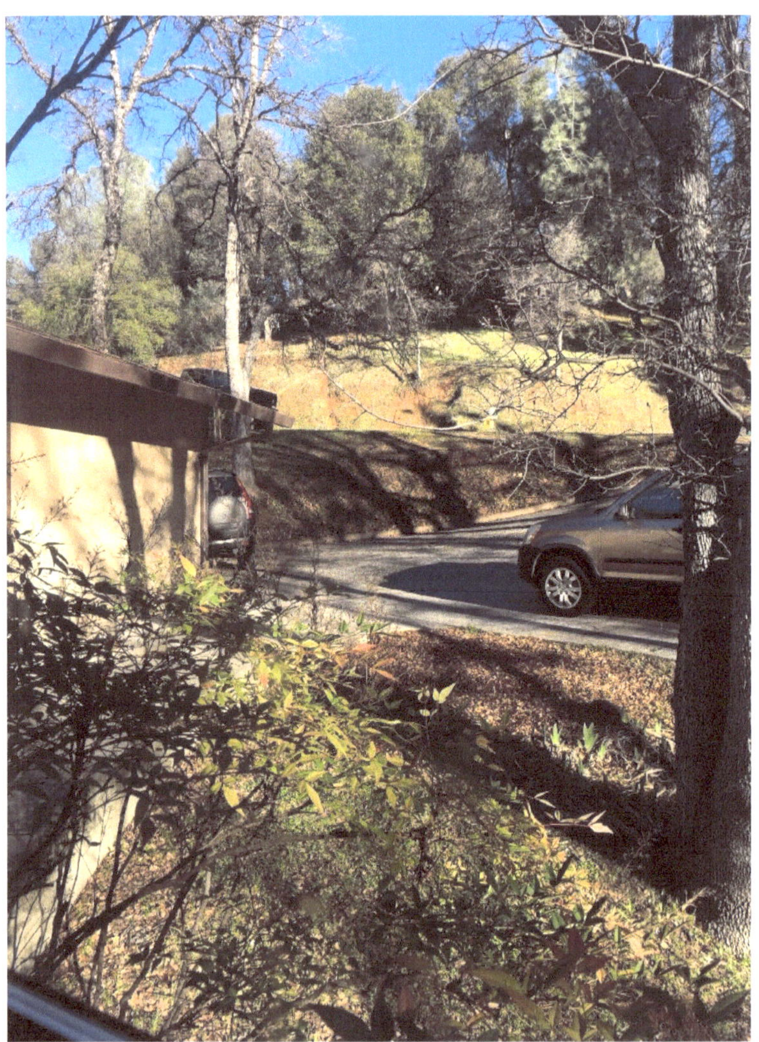

Figure 30--A PLACE ON A HILL

Kamikaze Run

Action
breezes past me
in shrouded streaks of skis
and speed-blurred rainbow clothes,
racing down
the slope.
This crumpled heap
is loathe to rise, but must,
to join the mind-blowing action
below

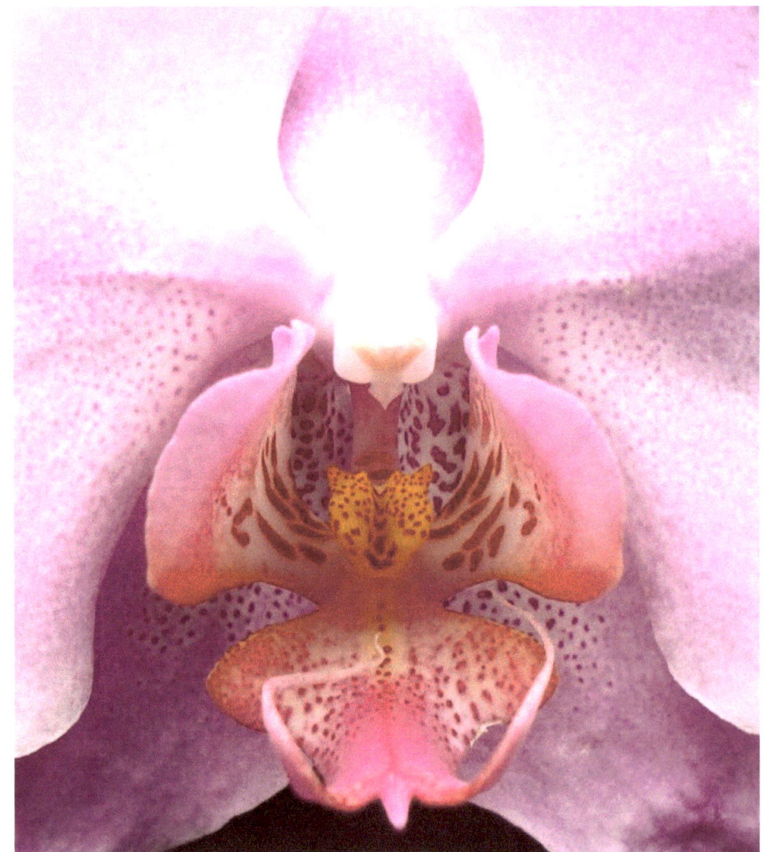

Figure 31--SIMPLY MAGIC

Cascade

Passion
before the storm
of deeds that lead to love
and nights to reinforce the heart,
billows

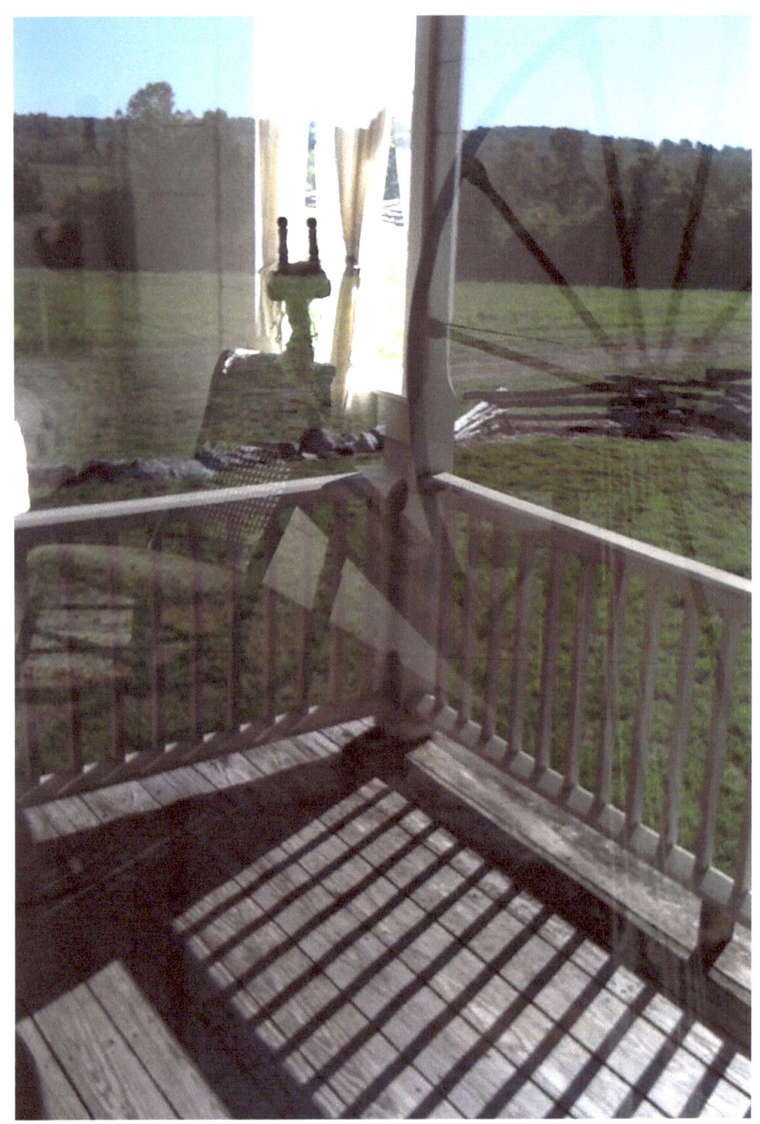

Figure 32--WAR WAS FOUGHT HERE, PEACE WAS WON

Lull

No chill
on the prairie,
dormant, awaiting white,
no wind to strip the illusion
of calm

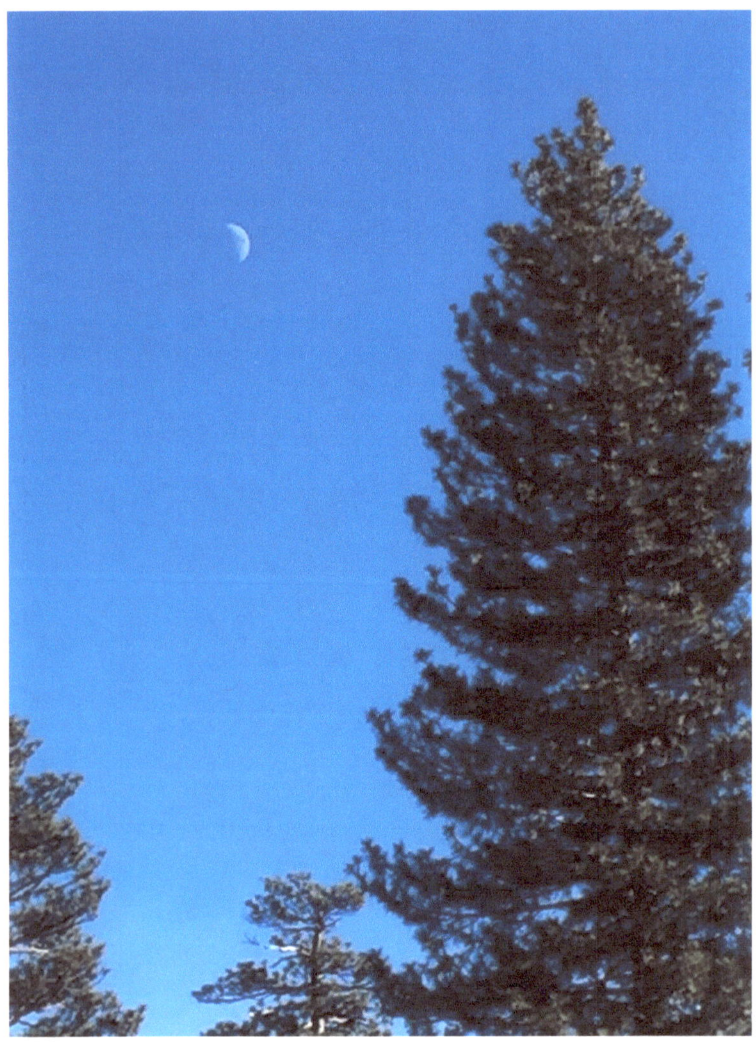

Figure 33--THE DEPTH OF A DREAM

Insight

Tickle
a “funny bone”
or a “flight of fancy”
into worlds we cannot yet see—
dream on

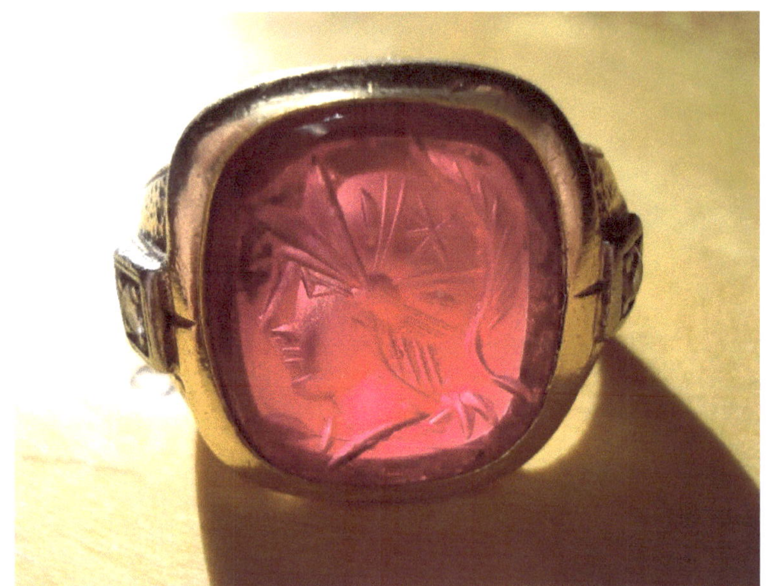

Figure 34--PRECIOUS IN SO MANY WAYS

Flushed Gem

Ruby,
ruddy healer
of southeast Asian birth
sparks vitality and passion,
bright red

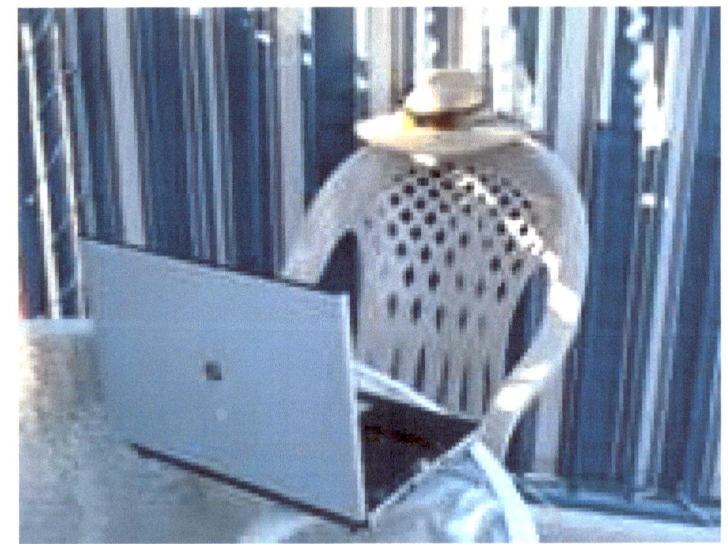

Figure 35--NOW YOU SEE ME

Quid Pro Quo

Joint creaks,
very pleasant
after working all day
sparking synapses to warp speed,
inspire
words on paper
while aches and pains linger
praying I'll break to lubricate
their needs

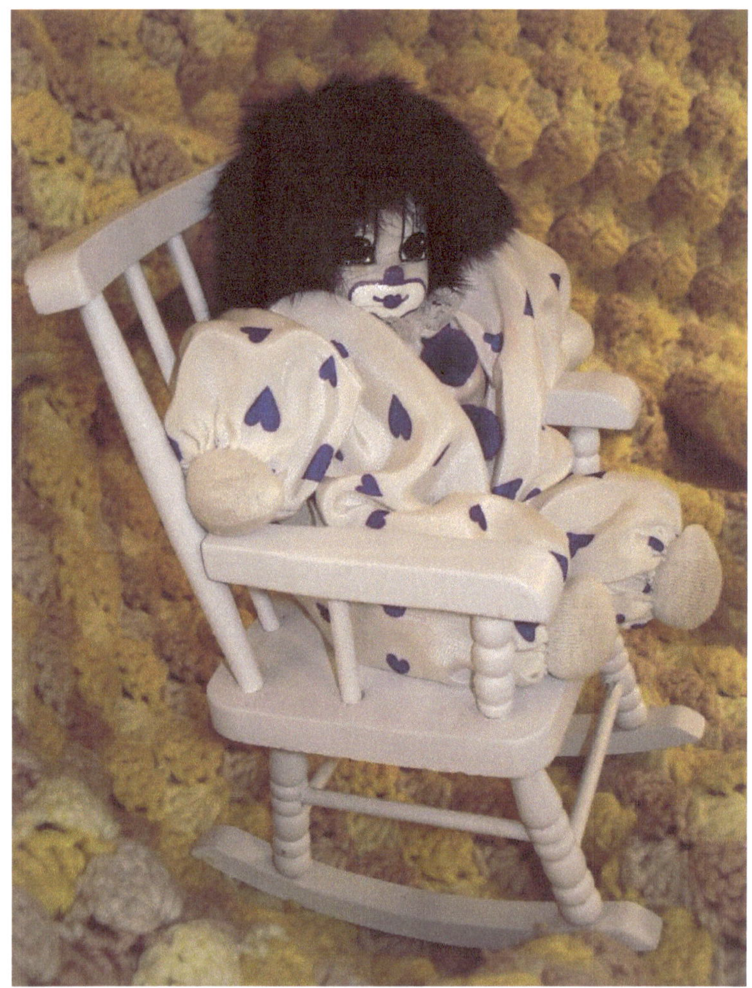

Figure 36—FASCINATING

Rock-A-Bye Clown

Puffy
clown rocks to sleep,
gaudy colors to greet
whimsical dreams of performance
visions
children rooted
to her practiced moves
of lavender polka dot blurs,
her joy

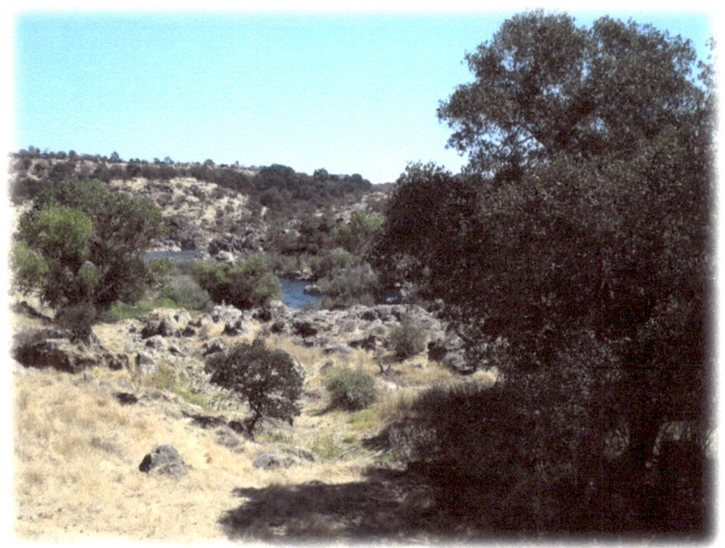

Figure 37--SO MANY WAYS TO GET LOST

Killdeer Lament

Speckled
egg in pressed grass
chills while a wild killdeer
calls insistent misdirection—
No, here!

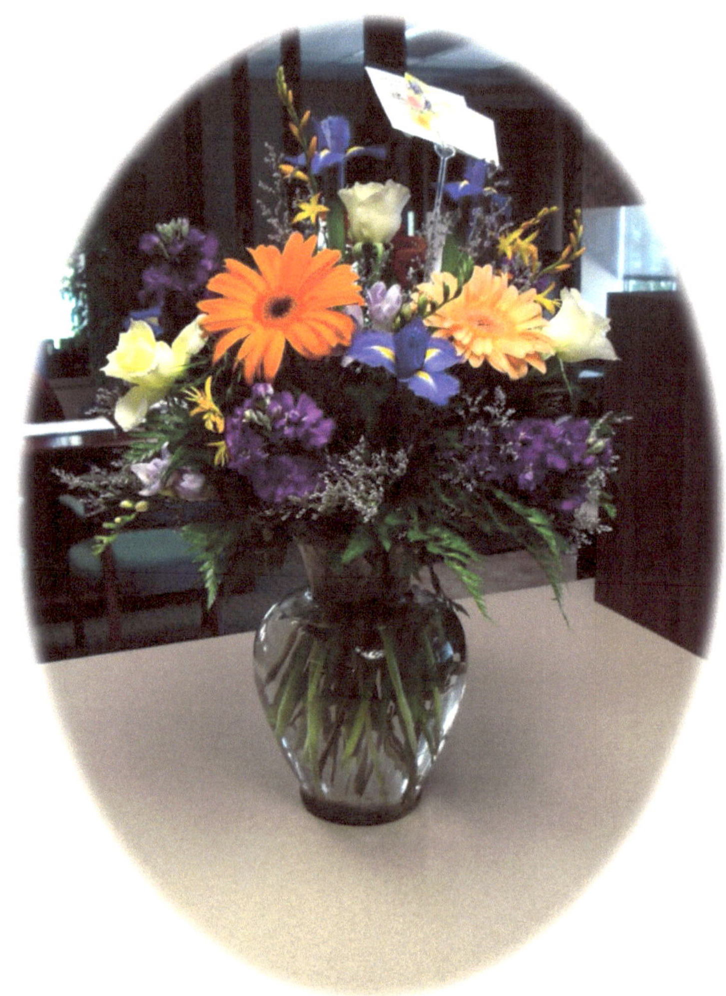

Figure 38--SPECIAL DELIVERY

Love is the Occasion

True love
expressed just right
on a card for your eyes
to grace, with St Valentine’s day
flowers

INDEX OF FIRST LINES

Ruby
Joint creaks
Puffy
Speckled
True love

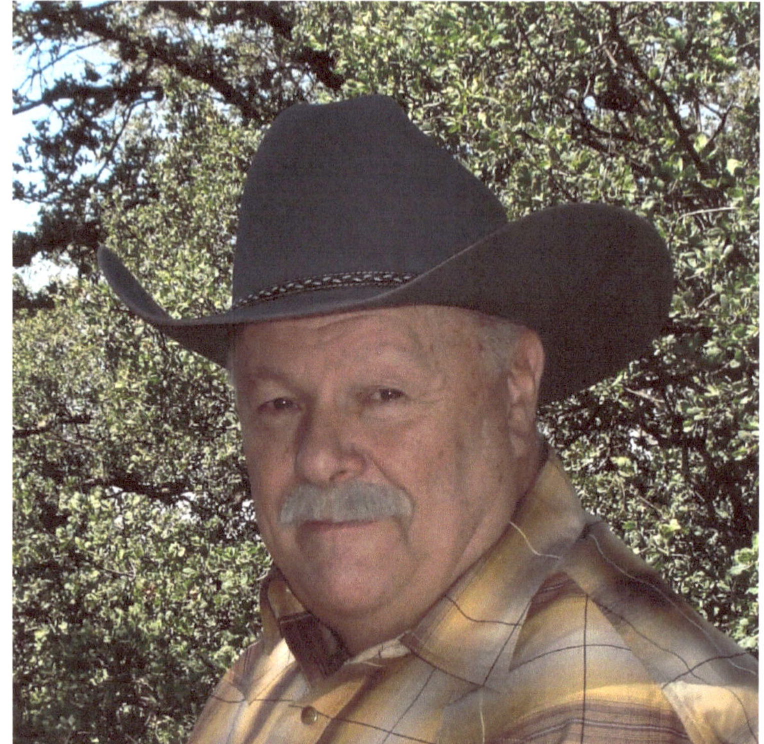

A native of California, a graduate of Missouri State University, and a globe-trotting student of mankind, Jim has taken the myriad inspirations and applied them to novels (Sport of Hearts, Kid Me You Die), a 1999 Win-Win Persie Award winner. His immensely popular books, Scattered Reflections and A Plea to a Wine Cork have given us poetic magic. Daydreams Alongside Surf promises to do it again, this time in a stream of cinquain and butterfly cinquain poems. He is currently developing a television SCI-FI pilot, Killigan.

www.ingramcontent.com/pod-product-compliance
Lightning Source LLC
LaVergne TN
LVHW052256100826
845147LV00001B/62

* 9 7 8 0 9 9 7 8 0 0 3 4 0 *